PRAISE FOR

love letter to the milky way

Statement by a Member of Congress to former Vice President Al Gore, during Gore's testimony at Congressional climate change hearings, April 24, 2009:

"I want to relate to your struggle a few moments ago to come up with the right words to define this moment. Because we're all talking and asking questions based on the concerns that our current constituents raise with us about this measure. And I wonder, what if the future generations had a voice? And if people living in our districts in 2080, or 2090, could speak to us now, what would they be saying? I'll give you one piece of poetry, actually, that I think brings it up pretty well, by a fellow named Drew Dellinger. He says,

'it's 3:23 in the morning
and I'm awake
because my great great grandchildren
won't let me sleep
my great great grandchildren
ask me in dreams
what did you do while the planet was plundered?
what did you do when the earth was unraveling?'"
　　—Congresswoman Tammy Baldwin

"Drew Dellinger is one of the most creative, courageous and prophetic poets of his generation. I love his spirit. Don't miss him!"
　　—Cornel West

"Drew Dellinger is a deep and courageous poet. How lucky we are!"
   —Alice Walker

"The poetry of Drew Dellinger is in the tradition of Walt Whitman with his panoramic eroticism but it's amped up even higher with the electricity from hip hop and the unquenchable passion of a Martin Luther King Jr., and the cosmic serenity of an Albert Einstein. When you're in the mood to have a torch put to your soul, Drew's the man."
   —Brian Swimme, author of *The Hidden Heart of the Cosmos*

"These poems are alive, kinetic, wily, as in artful, witty, wonderful sonic blasts, messengers of transformation. I am grateful for this young and powerful voice among us."
   —Susan Griffin, author of *Woman and Nature*

"Drew Dellinger has the Gift."
   —Richard Tarnas, author of *Cosmos and Psyche*

"Drew Dellinger is a national treasure. His poems for global justice bring light to these leaden times, helping us to see and defend the beauty of our world. His spoken word performances are exquisite in their intelligence and artistry: Setting the political challenges we face within the grandeur of our unfolding universe, they ignite both our wonder and our will."
   —Joanna Macy, author of *World As Lover, World As Self*

'One of the important voices of the global justice movement.'
   —*YES!* magazine

"Drew is the Earth's grapevine, the transcendent delivery man, the vocable giver, the dispatcher of the unremembered, the confabulating oath keeper, the stand-in for the intimate grief that holds us in thrall. His poems are bodies of light seen by startled new eyes and long after he speaks they weave the unconscious, stitching us to our collective and uncertain future."
 —**Paul Hawken,** author of *Blessed Unrest* and *The Ecology of Commerce*

"In a war-ravaged world, Drew Dellinger's poetry is a balm in Gilead. His unwavering commitment to truth telling and bearing witness is what the best of the prophetic tradition is made of. He is the poet laureate of the global democracy movement."
 —**Reverend Osagyefo Sekou**

"Drew Dellinger is one of the most respected and admired performers in the field of deep ecology / awakening / planetary work."
 —**Rob Hopkins,** founder of the Transition Town movement, Devon, UK

"Drew Dellinger is a master wordsmith who reframes the environmental movement in the vastness of cosmology."
 —**Leonora Oppenheim,** writer for *TreeHugger*, London, UK

"Thomas Berry insisted on the over-arching importance of spreading the epic version of the universe story as our new creation myth, and Thomas insisted that we couldn't leave this vital work of cultural therapy to scientists but must enlist the artists, musicians and poets. Well Drew Dellinger was among the first to answer this call and certainly among the most talented and effective. I can't speak highly enough of the quality of both the work and his delivery."
 —**John Seed,** rainforest activist and co-author of *Thinking Like a Mountain,* Sydney, Australia

"Dellinger is an electrifying, cosmopoetic presence as he whirls through galaxies, cuts across time, spirals into subatomic structures, stops on a nanosecond, rhymes and listens. Listen–he's crossing M.L. King with Thomas Berry, Teilhard de Chardin with hip hop. His great-great-grandchildren speak to him in dreams that will make your heart stop."

   —**China Galland,** author of *Love Cemetery, Unburying the Secret History of Slaves*

"Drew's poetry catapults us out of the sleep of conditionality. It is a clarion call that reawakens our primordial memory that we are made of the stuff of stars, along with our responsibility to care, ever so tenderly and passionately, for the cosmic majesty with which we have been entrusted."

   —**Michael Bernard Beckwith,** author of *Spiritual Liberation~Fulfilling
   Your Soul's Potential*

"Drew Dellinger is one of the most inspired poets of his generation and a troubadour for all who seek a world of justice, generosity, compassion and peace."

   —**Rabbi Michael Lerner,** Editor *Tikkun* and Chair, The Network of Spiritual
   Progressives

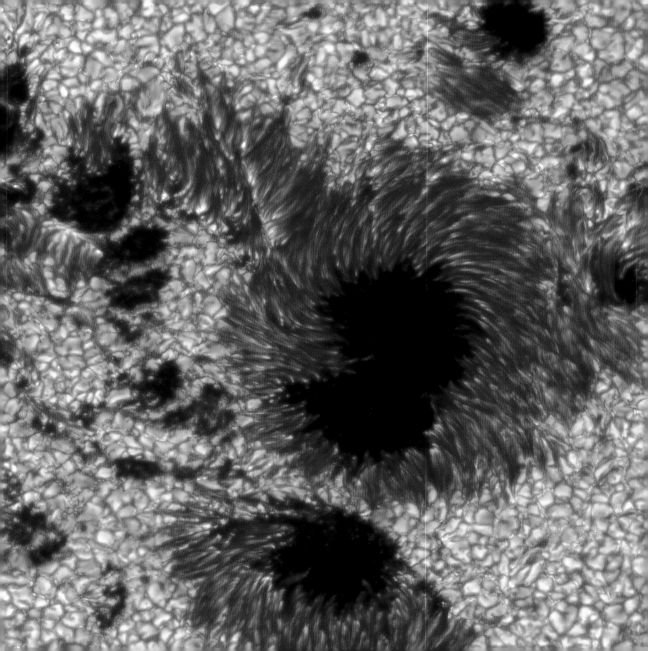

love letter to the milky way

a book of poems

drew dellinger

White Cloud Press
Ashland, Oregon

White Cloud Press, PO Box 3400, Ashland, OR 97520
www.whitecloudpress.com

Originally published 2002 by Planetize the Movement Press
Reprinted 2004. Expanded 2nd edition published 2007.
Reprinted 2010.

First White Cloud Press edition: 2011

Design by Amy Woloszyn & Drew Dellinger
Cover design and typesetting by Amy Woloszyn
www.amymade.com

All images (except pp. 4, 42) © Kevin W. Kelley 2011
Back cover photograph © Phyllis Christopher 2011

Printed in China

Library of Congress Cataloging-in-Publication Data

Dellinger, Drew, 1969-
 Love letter to the Milky Way : a book of poems / Drew Dellinger.
    p. cm.
 ISBN 978-1-935952-54-1 (pbk.)
 I. Title.
 PS3604.E4448L68 2011
 811'.6--dc22
                              2011025910

To
Thomas Berry
(1914 – 2009)

Foreword
by Matthew Fox

This poet speaks of a new heart, a new view, that a new cosmology brings in its wake. He speaks to our hearts and minds and passions with images and lessons our species needs desperately to hear. He puts heart into the new universe story and speaks passion from its depths. He speaks truth when he offers fresh critique of a misguided culture where "kids are raised to have Nike engraved on their psyche" and we "travel in and out of the veil of tears." He explains what made Buddha smile and how religion comes as stones and rivers and how bliss happens but also "collusion with illusion" and asks: "oh say can you see?" warning us that democracy has been "genetically modified" and "is at a crossroads of lost dreams and lost votes." And how "the capital of government has succumbed to the government of capital."

Drew Dellinger is mystic and prophet calling us to be the same and thus to be sane… again. He knows the stakes that our species is playing with at this perilous time in planetary and cultural history.

Foreword
by Thomas Berry

There is both grandeur and intimacy in these poems of Drew Dellinger; the grandeur of experiencing the far reaches of the universe beyond the stars, the intimacy of human affection in the immediacies of the present. The one is the measure of the other. If in the day we find ourselves in each other, at night the sky enfolds us to itself as we sleep, then greets us with the dawn as we awaken. We are children, not simply of Earth, we are children of the Milky Way, children of a mythic magical world wonderful beyond our dreams. Drew Dellinger brings us graciously into these experiences with the quiet yet insistent rhythms of his verse.

contents

hieroglyphic stairway

it's 3:23 in the morning
and I'm awake
because my great great grandchildren
won't let me sleep
my great great grandchildren
ask me in dreams
what did you do while the planet was plundered?
what did you do when the earth was unraveling?

surely you did something
when the seasons started failing?

as the mammals, reptiles, birds were all dying?

did you fill the streets with protest
when democracy was stolen?

what did you do
once
you
knew?

I'm riding home on the Colma train
I've got the voice of the milky way in my dreams

I have teams of scientists
feeding me data daily
and pleading I immediately
turn it into poetry

I want just this consciousness reached
by people in range of secret frequencies
contained in my speech

I am the desirous earth
equidistant to the underworld
and the flesh of the stars

I am everything already lost

the moment the universe turns transparent
and all the light shoots through the cosmos

I use words to instigate silence

I'm a hieroglyphic stairway
in a buried Mayan city
suddenly exposed by a hurricane

a satellite circling earth
finding dinosaur bones

in the Gobi desert
I am telescopes that see back in time

I am the precession of the equinoxes,
the magnetism of the spiraling sea

I'm riding home on the Colma train
with the voice of the milky way in my dreams

I am myths where violets blossom from blood
like dying and rising gods

I'm the boundary of time
soul encountering soul
and tongues of fire

it's 3:23 in the morning
and I can't sleep
because my great great grandchildren
ask me in dreams
what did you do while the earth was unraveling?

I want just this consciousness reached
by people in range of secret frequencies
contained in my speech

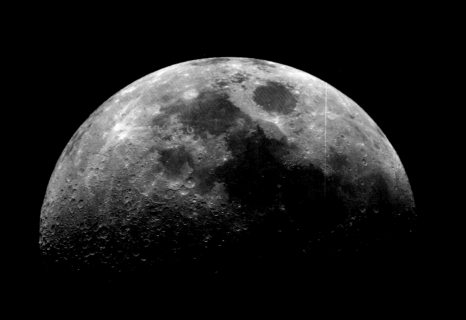

moon

luminous moon,
heavenly pearl,
circumnavigate the heartbroke cosmos–
reflect the lonely stars verbatim

curvature caressing
the sensate night

you can't hide your halo from me

like the moon,
we hide half of ourselves

beautiful moon,
show me your dark side

come to me shimmering, luminous

come to me
cradled in darkness

wait until the sunset
lights a path across the ocean;
walk to me

she who hears the cries of the world

the church of no return,
the fiery flesh of the original moment

dark madonna,
the beyond within us

words
kiss
stars
i
hope

even the full moon hides half of herself

luminous moon,
show me your dark side

the sun

the Sun
incandescent sphere
permanent explosion
its core
pouring itself out for us
source
to a hamlet of planets,
asteroids and comets
human trajectory
unfolds in this orbit
between wandering stars
and the invincible Sun

imagine when the heart of the Sun
goes supernova
instantly swallowing the distance
between us
the wet earth
a single tear
will finally merge with your fiery body

I've felt your heart beat
since the universe was plasma

ancient always new perpetual dawning
horizon of light
and arcing shadow
string of days and nights
primeval rhythm

the sky and the earth are lovers
who've been forced apart
earth yearns for the sky
clouds long to kiss ocean
mountains rise up with desire

Himalaya, Appalachia, Sierra, Shasta, Fuji, Kenya, Denali

the cosmos: a journey
the universe: longing

each human: a body of water

sunlight enters a drop of water
and disperses
into colors, sunlight
enters planet earth and species blossom

sacred secret

granite, sequoia, redwood, oak,
salamander, condor, beetle

radiant Sun
earth your disciple
apostle with strange powers
to manifest the mystery

the changing moon: a triple goddess
silver bow of Artemis
becomes
full moon
becomes
the goddess of the dark
moon
wandering
among souls of the dead
announced by howling dogs
she dwells on tombs
and lonely places where two roads
cross

every prophet
must make peace
with death

a sacred secret

imagine when your heart
goes supernova
blazing matter extending across 93 million
miles,
the wet earth
a single tear
will finally merge with your fiery body

golden light in cobalt sky
illumination of spaciousness
blue like Krishna's blue body
blue like the cosmos

love letter to the milky way

I want to tell you about love
There are approximately 1 trillion galaxies
I want to tell you about
In the Milky Way there are about 100 billion stars
I want to tell you
Love is the breath of the cosmos

I want to write a love letter to the Milky Way

Everything is an expression of the galaxy
My 30 trillion cells
The four noble truths
The eight-fold path
The five precepts
The seven energy centers of the body
Everything is the Milky Way
including my lover,
and every kiss
of every lover that's ever
lived

The deep sky
The ubiquity of spirit
The DNA of dreams
The interlocking patterns of the cosmic constellations

"Cosmos" and "justice" are synonymous with beauty
but parts of the Milky Way don't give off light
Sometimes it feels like I've got Ground Zero in my heart

The dark sun bleeds shadows
The dark sun leaves shadows on everything
The forecast calls for scattered to broken skies

If there wasn't so much love there wouldn't be so much pain
It's like love is the nervous system of the universe
bringing us joy and sorrow

I inherit the
voice of the Milky Way in my dreams
The entire galaxy revolves around a single drop of wine

Your skin
the texture of the cosmos
the religion beyond religion
I want to know you like the wind knows the canyons
or the rain knows the rivulets
Lightning is continuously striking in 100 places every moment
The universe spills through our dreams
The future belongs to the most compelling story
Even the word "love"
is not adequate to define
the force that wove
the fabric of
space/time

If we could sense everything at once
like Krishna entering history with all the memory of his past incarnations
then I could tell you about love

the laws of earth and objects

at the core of the Milky Way there's a black hole with a ring of blue
stars around it
at the core of the Milky Way there's a black hole with a ring of blue
stars around it

does anyone else feel this strange music?

'cause these days
kids are raised
with television the real religion
kids are raised with
television the real religion
kids are raised
to have Nike™
engraved
on their psyche

i travel in and out the veil of tears

that balcony in Memphis
in my eyes
gunshot in my ears
in a land of weary dreams

i travel in and out the veil of tears

i take the poison from the poison
turn the poison into passion
i take the poison
from
the poison
turn the poison into passion

i have no sister
but the moon
and the story of the oceans
and the blood of Christ like
music in my veins

i wander this
mountainous
aquatic
body of the goddess
tasting the
bread of the present
and the
breath of compassion

i want to know the laws of earth and objects
like patterns of migration
like the boiling point of water
like the law that holds the moon
so
gently

does anyone else feel this strange music?

lifetimes

I was born
in the eye of a storm
with no moon in the sky
between midnight
and dawn.
When I was young
I studied the transits of the planets
with sky watchers on Atlantis.
I saw alphabets
taking flight
from the winged silhouettes
of birds against the sky.
I wrote odes
to Osiris
on the very first sheet
of papyrus.
I was the only man allowed
on the Island of Lesbos
and each morn
Sappho would pin a poem
to my bedpost.
I went miles past the last
known fringe.

I drank psychedelic fluids with Druids
at Stonehenge,
then battled devils
on nine different levels
of hell,
that were made in
the crater when
Lucifer fell.
I've been on binges
smoking ganja by the Ganges
with some ninjas.
I've seen evil men do
I couldn't begin to
describe.
I've prayed with Hindu
Brahmins
and the shamans
of every tribe,
from Israelite to Shiite, Greek or Celtic
to Zulu to Zuni to Saxon or Toltec.
I've seen whole armies
commanded to wait
while I taught tactics
to young
Alexander the Great,

and the fact is,
when I think of my life,
it's hieroglyphics
to hip hop
in the blink of an eye.

I've had lifetimes
to write rhymes.
I've had lifetimes
to write rhymes
and get my game tight,
then waited to be incarnated
'til they invented
the mic.

...and life
twists and fades   like
smoke in the stage   lights...

You know how many times I've
drawn my last breath?
At this point
I just point
and straight
laugh at death.

I brought ayahuasca to Lhasa
for the 10th Dalai Lama,
told tales to Ali Baba,
and broke down fables
for knights at round tables.
I studied phonetics and mathematics
with ascetics and fanatics.
I told a circle of
men that was
making a declaration
of independence
to watch out
'cause
the premise is
white male
supremacist.
I took political science from Machiavelli,
was a poetic disciple of Michael Cirelli,
and to transcend
time and space we
go see
Taalam Acey.
I got the gift of gab
from the ghost of Christmas past.
I passed through Nazareth,
asked Jesus to please

check on Lazarus.
I took excursions with Persians
that eventually drew me
to slam poems
with Shams
of Tabriz
and then Hafiz,
and Rumi.
I sat in silence for six years
to clear out the mind
then ran into three more Temptations
on cloud nine,
and from there, I swear,
I could see a
heavenly band
of seventy angels
singing backup
for Aaliyah

…'cause life
twists and fades   like
smoke in the stage   lights…

I've had limitless
lifetimes.
I've had limitless
lifetimes
to write rhymes
and get my game tight,
then waited to be incarnated
'til they invented
this
mic.

...and life
twists and fades   like
smoke in the stage   lights...

Rumi

Rumi
the first whirling
saint of poetry
spinning
like a galaxy
weaving constellations of
words like blazing
stars, numinous moons
planets with gardens blossoming
and oceans floating in space.

Rumi
the first whirling saint of poetry
traversing
the geography
of divine desire with
longing stronger than the undertow of history.

This Presence is
mysterious, like the silhouette of music,
the circumference of a dream.

When Rumi met Shams
the clouds couldn't keep quiet
they cried at the question
that knocked Rumi down
they floated more slowly,
hoping to hear
whispers from
their mystical
conversations.

Rumi
sending words like flaming arrows
to penetrate hearts cold as
that December night
when Shams was called
to the back door
never to be
seen again.

Rumi
bathed in sacred graces
Rumi
bathed in sacred graces
like the wind that fills the flute
with notes of longing.

I saw Rumi
spinning verses
in the early morning hours,
one arm wrapped around the pillar,
his free hand tracing
outlines of angels in the air
songs with the power
to intoxicate prophets
longing for the Beloved
whose absence fills the world
invisible odes
built of breath
like God could kiss your lips
and transmit words that ride on waves
of how it feels when you're together.

is she radiant?

is she radiant?

she's the Sun's
little sister

her skin?

smoother than
the lily in
Georgia O'Keefe's
mind

her lips curve
around a word
like justice

damn, if I knew her better
I would tell her:
you are goddess
of the night sky
cloaked in humility
sweet as the knowledge of death
you are beautiful
sacred involution
the divine
folded into
your thought, breath, emotions

for one instant to be one with her becoming
to be close to her unfolding
to be near her blossoming
for one instant to be one with her becoming

with seeds in her pocket she
travels through the city
the cycles of the moon in her womb
thoughts of freedom on her tongue

with seeds in her pocket she
travels through the city her
hair dark
as the
crow-black night

is she radiant?

she's the Sun's
little sister

her skin?

smoother than
shadows,
and
sweet
like
desire

hymn to the sacred body of the universe

let's meet
at the confluence
where you flow into me
and one breath
swirls between our lungs

let's meet
at the confluence
where you flow into me
and one breath
swirls between our lungs

for one instant
to dwell in the presence of the galaxies
for one instant
to live in the truth of the heart
the poet says this entire traveling cosmos is
"the secret One slowly growing a body"

two eagles are mating–
clasping each other's claws
and turning cartwheels in the sky
grasses are blooming
grandfathers dying
consciousness blinking on and off

all of this is happening at once
all of this, vibrating into existence
out of nothingness

every particle
foaming into existence
transcribing the ineffable

arising and passing away
arising and passing away
23 trillion times per second–
when Buddha saw *that,*
he smiled

16 million tons of rain are falling every second
on the planet
an ocean
perpetually falling
and every drop
is your body
every motion, every feather, every thought
is your body
time
is your body,
and the infinite
curled inside like
invisible rainbows folded into light

every word of every tongue is love
telling a story to her own ears

let our lives be incense
burning
like a hymn to the sacred
body of the universe
my religion is rain
my religion is stone
my religion reveals itself to me in
sweaty epiphanies

every leaf, every river,
every animal,
your body
every creature trapped in the gears
of corporate nightmares
every species made extinct
was once
your body

10 million people are dreaming
that they're flying
junipers and violets are blossoming
stars exploding and being born
god

is having
déjà vu
I am one
elaborate
crush
we cry petals
as the void
is singing

you are the dark
that holds the stars
in intimate
distance

that spun the whirling,
whirling,
world
into existence

let's meet
at the confluence
where you flow into me
and one breath
swirls between our lungs

ancestors & angels

I write words to catch up to the ancestors.
An angel told me the only way
to walk through fire
without getting burned
is to become fire.
Some days angels whisper
in my ear as I walk
down the street and I fall in love
with every person I meet,
and I think, maybe this
could be a bliss
like when Dante met
Beatrice.
Other days all I see
is my collusion
with illusion.
Ghosts of projection
masquerading
as the radiant angel
of love.
You know I feel like
the ancestors
brought us together.

I feel like the ancestors
brought us here and they
expect great things.
They
expect us to say what
we think and
live how
we feel and follow the hard paths
that bring us near joy.
They expect us
to nurture
all the children.

I write poems to welcome angels
and conjure ancestors.
I pray to the angels of politics
and love.
I pray for justice sake
not to be relieved of my frustrations,
at the same time burning sage
and asking ancestors for patience.
I march with the people
to the border
between nations
where

everything stops
except
the greed of corporations.

Thoughts like comets
calculating the complexity
of the complicity.

There is so much noise in the oceans
the whales can't hear each other.
We're making them crazy,
driving dolphins insane.
What kind of ancestors
are we?

Thoughts like comets
leaving craters
in the landscape of my consciousness.

I pray to ancestors and angels:

Meet me in the garden.
Meet me where spirit walks softly
in the cool of the evening.
Meet me in the garden

under the wings of the bird
of many colors.
Meet me
in the garden
of your longing.

Every breath
is a pilgrimage.

Every
breath
is a pilgrimage
to you.

I pray
to be
a conduit.

An angel told me:

the only way
to walk through fire–

become fire.

the total thrust is global justice

The total thrust is
global justice
so we gotta fix the politics
and put a check upon its economics
or before you know it, a warrior-poet
may try to upend the
corporate agenda that's
got 'em blind to the real bottom line.
It's intense when you sense the only interests
on the docket
are fat cats with Republi-Crats
in their pocket.
It's crooked now
just look at how
the pundits are funded.
They're devious at CBS and, yes,
they'll choose the news that fits the script unless
I play tricks on the matrix.
(In case you can't guess shit,
I'm not to be messed with.)
The folks know my art form
comes straight from the heart for 'em.
A lyrical storm that departs from the norm

and transforms as I'm giving
rhymes for the minds in the times that we live in.
I can't hang with the anguish
and I don't want my language to languish
'cause there ain't nothing like Drew's
hip hop haikus
I got a mandate
to disturb
the urban landscape.

We got tyrannies
right here in these
States,
and you never know
when they'll go
right back to some tactics
like COINTELPRO.
If we could see through the lies
see how they brutalize
and get cops
to beat speech in the streets
and guard sweatshops.
I'm ending these industries.
Please can we factor the
effect of the

trajectory.
This whole place is racist
and sexist from North
Dakota down to Texas
with the twenty-first century's
youth in penitentiaries
and the night never seemed this dark
but now half of the stars
are behind prison bars.
Oh say can you see?
But if we can dream a new day it may be.
You had to know the baddest bro
with the phattest flow would shake up the status quo
with my adjectives and adverbs and ad libs.
Like Gandhi
protest is my *modus operandi.*
It's like Malcolm and Martin's
evolution with art
and revolution
'cause the total thrust is
global justice.

Attention, Shoppers!

performed at the mass demonstration, "Another World is Possible,"
counter-protest to the World Economic Forum, New York City, Feb. 2, 2002

In every nation
we're losing patience
with corporations,
'cause who knows
what all they're in on:
Arms.
Oil.
Enron.
But since the Earth,
and the people
can't take too much more I'm
bound to put a check upon
this economic forum.

It's time to reject the hypocrisy,
connect direct democracy
so I drop my philosophy
at terminal velocity.

We need to be wary or
every year it gets scarier
now justice just is a barrier
to their free trade area,
and freedom
is no longer
cost effective—

Attention, shoppers!
Freedom
is no longer cost effective—

Attention, shoppers!
Democracy
has been genetically modified

By corporations
filing suit
for the right
to pollute.
In the name of
free trade
trying to pave
over laws that
we made?

To capitalize
on the new world order,
militarize
the border.
Now the media's
corporate
so every report gets
distorted.
We need a rebel alliance.
We need a new level of defiance.
Since the Earth,
and the people
can't take too much more I'm
bound to put a check
upon this economic forum!

Attention, shoppers!
Freedom
is no longer cost effective–

Attention, shoppers!
Democracy
has been genetically modified

democracy's at a crossroads

performed at Presidential Inauguration counter-protest,
January 20, 2001, Oakland, CA

Democracy's at a crossroads
of lost dreams and lost votes,
so hell yes I'm contesting the election,
requesting the rejection
of invalid blocks at the ballot box.

Weakass leaders speak as
cheaters seek to eke
out victory,
bend the
laws in their favor
and reality bites like the
jaws of a gator.

The corporate, right-wing, pathetic,
mainstream media try to
confound it,
when the issue at hand is
thousands of votes that couldn't be cast
or haven't been counted.

The combination of this
and the lies meant
disenfranchisement.

It's hard to be awed
by how far we've
come when we
are still crossing
that bridge
from Selma
to Montgomery.

With respect to these inequities
all the Supreme Court can say is
too bad, so sad
and leave me hangin'
like chad.

I need a reprieve
and you better believe
I think this
court
is out of order
I'm doubting Thomas,
Scalia,

Rehnquist.
I take issue with pre/judicial officials,
because their heart is in
the partisan
all out war, voting 5-4
to deprive Gore
what I saw was raw
politics putting the fix
in like Nixon with tricks
in the sleeves of their
black robes
to back those
that lack
votes.

We need global
citizens for some sit-ins
again.
I say we all meet
on Wall Street
and lock down–
lock the whole block down!
I'll storm the White House
right now,
for real, I ain't havin' it.

I'll uproot Bush
and overturn the cabinet.
Then let's go
to death row
let's close
every jail in the nation, free a
whole generation,
plus Mumia.
I'm not joking,
we'll end in Oakland
with some
sit-ins on the dock of the Bay
like the Doc, MLK
watching the apartheid roll away.

I'm settin' precedents
the planetary poet-in-residence.
Call all the Justices—
call the President—
tell 'em Drew's comin' to get ya.
No, not to hurt ya
but to give you a lecture:
you can't elect yourself
that's rule one.
You're done son—

so let's go.
(We'll have your mom and your dad come get you
in the limo.)
Because democracy's at a cross
roads.
I get down at times
I'm surrounded
by hypocrisies,
but I took an oath to diagnose
like Hippocrates:
Democracy's at a crossroads
of lost dreams and lost votes.

magic bullet theory

we need a poet to slam some
new national anthem.
we need a poet to slam some
new national anthem.
'cause it's the time of the season
for rhyming with reason,
and treason creeps
when my peeps are all sleeping.
it's deep when
the corporate elite have been
cheatin'

and the main thing to know about war in Iraq is
Bush lied, people died, and all war is a racket.

an illegitimate president,
a prince of smoke and mirrors
who hasn't had a self-reflective moment
since his days of coke and mirrors

a stolen election
a suspicious attack
a cover-up
legislation hastily passed
a pre-planned agenda
a nebulous war
pre-emptive invasion
secret military courts

corporate media
too afraid to follow the facts
in these days of charades
and fake patriot acts.

a military-industrial-petroleum complex
that can cancel democracy
by calling in bomb threats

a single bullet somehow piercing every heart

but the truth is bulletproof
we need an open conspiracy
for freedom and democracy,
a transparent conspiracy
for justice and ecology

the truth is bulletproof
we need a team to confront a regime like King
and elevate the stakes like Ella Baker
we need a poet to slam some
new national anthem

to those who have suffered
much will be revealed
follow your tears
the future needs us
now.

re:vision

open your eyes.

see visions.

imagine a melody,

infinitely—

listen.

a planet of stories
with islands of silence,
her curved surface
radiates grace.

milky way blazing
in the sky above the city.
speaking in fractals,
the stars are telepathic

wake the poets.
wake the dreamers.

cultivate the tendrils
in the vineyard
of your heart

reorient our buildings to the solstice,
and from the center of the city,
see the stars.

soulstice

every ounce of matter is frozen light
roses, clouds, bones, tears
all slowly moving light

everything is shining in glory
everything
singing a story

if love is a language
then I am just
learning to spell
while there's a story
that the stars
have been
burning
             to tell

everything is blazing
like a diaphanous theophany

everything is shining
like the radiant mind
of a child
like the eyes of a saint
like the dawn on the Nile
where the pyramids
track the arc
of the spinning
earth

sometimes I wander the streets and curse
the darkness
with a heart that's
frozen
   as the
      arctic

while winds are forming
as the planet's turning
and I'm thinking
about 500 years of oppression
and I'm thinking
about 500 years of resistance
and I'm thinking:
what if the trade winds
had blown the other way?

would we not have been spared
the middle passage?

still I wander the streets and curse
the darkness
with a heart that's
frozen
        as the
                arctic

because the capital of government
has succumbed to the
government
of capital

but I know the longest night
gives way to the strongest light
so I prolong this fight
until what's
wrong
        is
           right

every second in the universe a supernova is
exploding
every second a star is shattering

and flames were
leaping off the moon
last night
flames were
leaping off the moon
last night

like binary stars we
circle
each other

like binary stars we
circle
each
other

and
the more I
see   of   you
the more I
love   the   view

let me be a fierce clear mirror
in a cosmos made of passions

let me be a fierce clear mirror
in a cosmos made of passions

open the window
let me feel the star-filled night

if you can stand before the cosmos
until your form becomes transparent
the stars will pour beams
through your
emancipated

borders, open the window
let me feel the star-filled night

if love is a language
then I am still
learning to spell
while there's a story
that the stars
have been
burning
to tell.

thanks...

...to everyone who's inspired and supported my poetry, including:

My family; Tracy Lee Jones; Belvie Rooks; Chapel Hill homies; Bay Area poets and spoken word family; Bay Area activists and organizers; Art & Revolution; the Challenging White Supremacy workshop; the Cosmic Mass; California Institute of Integral Studies; Omar Zinn; Stephan Snider; Danielle Drake-Burnette; William Burnette; Vaschelle André; Amy Woloszyn; Bien Concepcion; Kevin W. Kelley; Ben Galland; Deborah Harlow.

Special shout out to the Earth, the ancestors, my grandmother, Grace Dellinger, and my son, Israel Dellinger

gratitude for all the influences woven through these poems, especially:

Thomas Berry, Brian Swimme, Susan Griffin, Matthew Fox, Taalam Acey, Spoken Word, Hip Hop.

Special thanks to Thomas Berry (1914 – 2009) for his cosmological vision, his poetic perception of the Earth, his teaching, writing and mentoring, his authenticity and his friendship. For baptizing me into the presence of the galaxies and showing me the poetry of the planet.

Note: some phrases in "the sun" were adapted from language in *The Secret Language of the Stars and Planets*, by G. Cornelius & P. Devereux. (Chronicle, 1996)

drew dellinger, Ph.D., is an internationally sought-after speaker, poet, writer, and teacher who has inspired minds and hearts around the world, performing poetry and speaking on justice, ecology, cosmology, and compassion. He is also a consultant, publisher, and founder of Planetize the Movement (planetizethemovement.org).

Dellinger has presented at over 1000 events across the U.S., U.K., Canada, and Australia. He has spoken and performed at numerous conferences–including Bioneers, the Green Festival, the Dream Reborn, and the Parliament of the World's Religions–as well as colleges and universities, poetry venues, protests, and places of worship. He has shared podiums and stages with luminaries such as Alice Walker, Cornel West, Thomas Berry, Danny Glover, Julia Butterfly Hill, Brian Swimme, Paul Hawken, Ani Difranco, Chuck D, Eve Ensler, and many others.

Dellinger co-wrote the documentary film, "The Awakening Universe," which premiered at the United Nations. As a consultant, Dellinger helped develop and design the Pachamama Alliance's Awakening the Dreamer, Changing the Dream Symposium, now used in 54 countries, in 14 languages. In 1997 Dellinger received *Common Boundary* magazine's national Green Dove Award. In 2010 he received a *Writer's Digest* Book Award.

Dellinger has taught at Prescott College, Naropa University–Oakland, Esalen Institute, Sophia Center, and John F. Kennedy University, where he was Associate Professor and Director of the Program in Social Ecology. He studied cosmology and ecological thought with Thomas Berry for twenty years, and is currently writing a book on the cosmology of Martin Luther King Jr.

Dellinger has been called "a national treasure," by Joanna Macy, "a deep and courageous poet," by Alice Walker and "one of the most creative, courageous and prophetic poets of his generation," by Cornel West.

www.drewdellinger.org
info@drewdellinger.org
1-866-poetics (1-866-763-8427)